Lee Brickley's
Haunted Christmas

Eerie Yuletide Tales from the World's Most Mystical Corners

Copyright @ Lee Brickley 2023

Contents:

Introduction..5

The Ghost of Christmas Past...9

The Mistletoe Apparition...13

The Caroling Specters of New England..17

The Yuletide Banshee in Irish Countryside...21

The Phantom Sleigh Bells of Siberia..25

Santa's Spectral Visit in Melbourne...29

The Christmas Eve Poltergeist of Prague..33

The Cursed Christmas Market of Bavaria...39

The Lost Carolers of Canterbury..45

The Yule Lads' Haunting of Icelandic Winters.......................................49

The Bewitched Christmas Tree of Nova Scotia......................................53

The Disappearing Ornaments of Oslo...57

The Christmas Goblin of Greece..61

The Ghostly Procession in Colonial Williamsburg................................65

The Haunting Hum of Helsinki..69

The Haunted Advent Calendar of Vienna...73

The Shrouded Specter of Shanghai's Silent Night.................................77

A Scottish Christmas: The Eerie Encounter on the Loch..................81

The Possessed Puppet Show of Rome's Piazza Navona..................85

The Ghastly Guest at the Christmas Feast of Rio de Janeiro.........89

The Whispers of Warsaw's Snowfall..93

The Snowman of the Swiss Alps..97

The Phantom Carolers of Cape Town......................................101

The Eerie Echoes of Edmonton's Ice Castle.............................105

Yuletide Yokai: Christmas Spirits of Japan..............................109

The Bethlehem Phantom: The Holy Land's Christmas Ghost....113

Afterword...117

Introduction

As the cold winds sweep through the narrow cobblestone streets of my Staffordshire home, and the soft glow of fairy lights twinkle from frost-covered windows, I am once again reminded of the enchanting mystery that is Christmas. But it's not the charm of twinkling decorations, the warm hum of carols, or even the festive air of merriment that captivates me; no, my mind is drawn to the ethereal tales that lurk in the shadows of this Yuletide season, tales that lie waiting in the mystical corners of the world, each imbued with an eerie charm that only surfaces as the clock strikes midnight on Christmas Eve.

My name is Lee Brickley, and I am a paranormal investigator. For years, I've devoted my life to uncovering the inexplicable, the eerie, and the uncanny. From remote Scottish lochs shrouded in fog to the bustling cityscape of Shanghai, I've traversed the globe, untangling the world's most haunting mysteries. And yet, each year, as the seasons change and the scent of mulled wine and gingerbread fills the air, I am inexorably drawn back to the spectral phenomena of Christmas.

You might question, why focus on Christmas? What is it about this time of year that attracts these phantasmal tales? Is it the ancient Pagan traditions that echo in our modern celebrations? Or perhaps the veil between worlds grows thin as the year draws to a close? The truth is, I cannot say for certain. But I can tell you that the stories contained within these pages hold a unique allure that remains unseen during the rest of the year.

You will journey with me to Victorian London, where the ghost of Christmas past has more than metaphorical connotations. We'll stroll the romantically lit streets of Paris, only to encounter an unsettling apparition beneath a mistletoe's shade. From there, we'll travel to New England, where spectral figures take on the festive tradition of carol singing, their chilling melodies echoing across the frosty landscape.

Our journey will take us across continents and through time. From the Banshee's eerie wails in the Irish countryside to phantom sleigh bells in Siberia, from Santa's spectral visits in Melbourne to the Prague poltergeist disturbing a family's peace every Christmas Eve, we'll delve deep into these tales, shivering not from the winter chill but from the spine-tingling narrative these stories weave.

Christmas, as I have come to discover, is not merely a season of joy and togetherness but also a time when the spectral and mysterious emerge, adding their otherworldly whispers to the festive cheer. Every culture, every tradition, from the ghostly procession in Colonial Williamsburg to the Yuletide Yokai of Japan, has its unique spin on these uncanny occurrences.

Prepare to traverse the snowy streets of Bavaria where a cursed Christmas market stands, and explore the quaint town of Canterbury, haunted by the ghostly carolers who have long lost their way. We will delve into the folklore of the Icelandic Yule Lads, and unravel the mystery of a bewitched Christmas tree in Nova Scotia. From Greece's mischievous goblins to Rome's possessed puppet show, we're about to embark on a journey through the world's most haunted Yuletide.

My experiences have taught me that the line separating the material from the spectral is often blurry. These stories, each drawn from local lore, eyewitness accounts, and my investigations, serve as reminders of this fragile boundary. They beckon us to look deeper, to question, and to embrace the eerie beauty that dances in the shadows of the Yuletide.

So, as you settle down in your favourite chair, the soft glow of the Christmas tree illuminating these pages, I invite you to join me on this journey. Let us walk together through these haunted tales, where each chime of the church bell, each rustle of the Christmas wreath, might just signal the presence of something from the beyond.

Because remember, as we traverse through "Lee Brickley's Haunted Christmas: Eerie Yuletide Tales from the World's Most Mystical Corners," it is often in the chill of a silent, snowy night that the echoes of the spectral world ring the loudest.

Welcome, dear reader, and merry haunted Christmas.

Your guide in the shadows,

Lee Brickley.

The Ghost of Christmas Past

As the clock struck midnight on a foggy Christmas Eve, the dimly lit streets of Victorian London were blanketed with a stillness only the anticipation of Christmas Day could bring. But amidst the tranquillity, an eerie encounter was about to unravel, one that still sends shivers down the spines of Londoners and continues to be retold around glowing fireplaces on every Yuletide eve. This chilling tale is none other than that of the Ghost of Christmas Past, a Victorian phantom whose spectral presence is as much a part of London's Christmas as the glowing warmth of mince pies or the harmonious melodies of carolers.

It all began in 1843, the year Charles Dickens introduced the world to Ebenezer Scrooge. At the same time, a real-life drama was unfolding in an opulent Victorian home nestled in the heart of London. The dwelling, belonging to the prosperous Worthington family, was steeped in yuletide splendour, its grand halls adorned with boughs of holly and a resplendent Christmas tree gracing the drawing-room.

The Worthingtons were a picture of Victorian sophistication, well-respected within their social circles. But their affluence did little to shield them from the spectral presence that would forever alter their festive celebrations. For as the family nestled in their beds on Christmas Eve, waiting for the break of dawn and the joy it promised, a chilling wail echoed through their ornate corridors. The mournful cry, distinctly feminine, was interspersed with the phantom whispers of a song, a carol from another time. The ghostly spectacle left the family in a state of fearful wonder, the once warm yuletide atmosphere now tainted with an undercurrent of spectral apprehension.

Haunted by the inexplicable incident, the Worthingtons decided to investigate. Their search led them to an old maid in their employ, Agnes, who claimed to have had her own eerie encounters. As the story unfolded, it became evident that the Worthington home was not simply playing host to Christmas cheer but also to a ghostly inhabitant from Christmas past.

Agnes, a soft-spoken woman, spoke of an apparition that had frequented her dreams for weeks leading up to Christmas. She described a lady dressed in Victorian attire, her visage lined with a melancholic sorrow. The spectral woman would hum a quaint carol as she moved around the house, visible only to Agnes. The lady, Agnes explained, seemed to be searching for something, or perhaps, someone. Every night, the apparition would end her spectral journey at the grand Christmas tree, her ethereal figure slowly dissipating among the twinkling lights.

The Worthingtons, intrigued by the maid's account and desperate to understand the nature of their nocturnal visitor, sought the help of local spiritualists. Their investigation revealed a tale of lost love and Yuletide sorrow. The grand house, before becoming the Worthington home, belonged to a young woman named Eleanor. Eleanor was betrothed to a sailor who left for sea promising to return by Christmas. She spent that fateful Christmas Eve singing carols by their tree, waiting for her love who tragically never returned.

The spiritualist surmised that Eleanor's spirit was trapped in a cycle of perpetual Christmas Eves, her soul unable to move on due to her undying love. To help her, the family started a tradition of singing Eleanor's carol around the tree every Christmas Eve, a tradition the Worthingtons maintain to this day.

Over the years, several guests of the Worthington family have reported encountering Eleanor's apparition. Their accounts remain strikingly consistent – a lady in Victorian attire, humming a long-forgotten carol, her melancholic aura adding a ghostly charm to the Christmas festivities.

While the Ghost of Christmas Past might seem like a chilling spectre, her tale is a reminder of the poignant echoes of love and longing that often lie hidden beneath the jovial veneer of Christmas. Even in her spectral form, Eleanor is a testament to the human spirit's endurance, her tale adding a deeper layer of poignancy to London's Christmas celebrations. It's a haunting blend of Yuletide warmth and spectral chills that keeps this tale alive, a stark reminder of the thin veil separating our world from the one beyond.

As the story of the Ghost of Christmas Past continues to be told and retold, it transforms from mere folklore into a spectral tradition, a unique ghostly tapestry woven into the very fabric of London's Christmas. Today, on every Christmas Eve, when the clock strikes midnight and the city falls silent, those who listen closely might hear the faint echo of a long-forgotten carol. And in that moment, they'll know that Eleanor, the Ghost of Christmas Past, has returned for her annual Yuletide visit, a spectral presence adding her own haunting melody to London's Christmas symphony.

The Mistletoe Apparition

In the heart of Paris, nestled among historic boulevards and enchanting architecture, lies a tale that has fascinated paranormal enthusiasts and Yuletide lovers alike for generations. Known as "The Mistletoe Apparition," it weaves a complex tapestry of holiday cheer, ancient folklore, and spectral mystery.

Our story unfolds in a grand Parisian maison, just off the bustling Champs-Élysées. This mansion, La Maison de Noël, as it has come to be known, was built in the 19th century by a wealthy Parisian named Henri Moreau. An avid lover of Christmas, Moreau was known throughout the city for his extravagant Yuletide festivities. However, these grand celebrations were overshadowed by an otherworldly presence that would forever intertwine the Moreau home with Paris's spectral folklore.

The first recorded incident dates back to Christmas Eve of 1865. As the story goes, the Moreau family was hosting their annual

Christmas party. The mansion was resplendent, aglow with Yuletide cheer. A grand Christmas tree towered in the drawing room, its branches adorned with flickering candles and exquisite ornaments. Mistletoes were hung in doorways and hallways, a traditional symbol of love and friendship inviting guests to share a holiday kiss.

As the clock chimed midnight, signalling the arrival of Christmas Day, a hush fell over the attendees. In that silence, an ethereal figure materialised beneath a mistletoe hanging in the grand hallway. The apparition was described as a lady dressed in elegant Victorian attire, her face obscured by a lace veil. Her figure shimmered in the candlelight, giving her an almost ethereal glow. The crowd watched in stunned silence as the spectral figure floated silently across the hallway before vanishing into thin air.

In the days that followed, accounts of the eerie spectacle made their way through the streets of Paris, adding a chilling undertone to the city's Yuletide celebrations. Moreau, intrigued and somewhat unsettled by the apparition in his home, reached out to local spiritualists in an attempt to unravel the mystery.

As the investigation unfolded, the spectral woman beneath the mistletoe began appearing more frequently, often materialising at the stroke of midnight and vanishing with the dawn. Witnesses reported a peculiar detail—the apparition seemed drawn to the mistletoe, always appearing beneath its green sprigs and crimson berries.

Delving into the history of the mansion, the spiritualists unearthed a tale of lost love. The property once belonged to a young woman named Margot, who had been betrothed to a man lost at sea. Margot held on to the hope that her love would return by Christmas, and legend says she would wait beneath the mistletoe each Christmas Eve, anticipating a reunion that never came.

The spiritualists speculated that Margot's spirit lingered in the mansion, forever waiting for her lost love under the mistletoe. The Moreau family, moved by the tragic tale, started a tradition of hanging a mistletoe in the grand hallway every Christmas, a gesture for Margot to keep her vigil.

Over the years, accounts of the Mistletoe Apparition have continued. Witnesses describe a soft scent of roses accompanying her presence and a gentle rustle of mistletoe leaves, as if brushed by an unseen hand. Some have even claimed to hear a soft, melodic hum, akin to a woman singing a tender lullaby.

Though a haunting, the Mistletoe Apparition has become a beloved part of Paris's Yuletide lore, her spectral presence adding an eerie, yet poignant charm to the city's Christmas celebrations. The Moreau mansion, now known as La Maison de Noël, has become a hub for paranormal enthusiasts and holiday revellers alike, all drawn to the enduring tale of a love that transcends the veil of mortality.

As Christmas descends upon Paris, turning the City of Lights into a winter wonderland, the Mistletoe Apparition reminds us of the intertwining of joy and sorrow, love and loss, and the tangible and spectral that make up the fabric of our human experience. When the clock strikes midnight on Christmas Eve, and the soft scent of roses fills the grand hallway of La Maison de Noël, one can't help but spare a thought for Margot, the eternal romantic, waiting for her lost love beneath the mistletoe.

The Caroling Specters of New England

The hushed snowfall of a New England Christmas carries with it a haunting melody that has echoed through the centuries, a spectral chorus that adds an eerie harmony to the joyous carols of the holiday season. Welcome, dear reader, to the tale of the Caroling Specters of New England, a yuletide story cloaked in the shroud of the paranormal.

Our story is set in the quaint town of Northbridge, Massachusetts. Steeped in colonial history and rich with Christmas tradition, Northbridge is the epitome of festive New England charm. However, as the nights grow longer and the festive lights sparkle against the snow, an ethereal phenomenon takes hold of the town.

It began in the early 1800s, during the town's founding years. Christmas Eve had fallen upon Northbridge, its houses aglow with the warmth of yuletide celebrations. As the clock struck midnight, the town was suddenly filled with the hauntingly beautiful sound of carols sung in ethereal harmony. The townsfolk, stirred from their homes by the melodies, were astonished to see a group of spectral figures robed in colonial attire, their forms translucent in the snowy night, standing in the town square. These apparitions, ethereal in the moonlit snow, were the source of the melodic carols that echoed through Northbridge.

This event sparked a town-wide fascination, intrigue, and fear that has held sway over Northbridge ever since. Each Christmas Eve, as the midnight hour approaches, the town's inhabitants gather in the square, their breath misting in the chilly air, waiting for the spectral carolers to make their yuletide appearance.

Eyewitness accounts over the years have added depth and intrigue to the tale. Some claim to have seen the spectres close enough to discern their expressions, which were described as serene, their eyes seeming to look beyond the physical realm. Others have reported feeling a bone-chilling cold sweep over them as the apparitions materialise, followed by an inexplicable sense of peace as the ghostly choir begins its ethereal hymns.

In an attempt to understand the spectral phenomenon, local historians delved into the town's archives. The findings were as chilling as they were heartbreaking. During a particularly harsh winter in the 1700s, a group of early settlers succumbed to the cold while trying to reach the safety of the nearby settlement. Records show they were last seen on Christmas Eve. The historians theorised that these ill-fated settlers are the ghostly figures haunting the town square.

As the tale of the Caroling Specters of New England spread beyond Northbridge, the town became a beacon for paranormal enthusiasts and those intrigued by the spectral realm. And yet, amidst the chilling encounters and ghostly tales, the essence of the story has remained inherently linked to the spirit of Christmas.

The apparitions, with their hauntingly beautiful carols, serve as a spectral reminder of the resilience and unity inherent in the holiday season. They symbolise a bridge between the physical and ethereal realms, their melodies a poignant echo of a tragic past interwoven with the joyous celebration of Christmas.

The tale of the Caroling Specters is now part of the very fabric of Northbridge, a chilling yet beautiful part of its yuletide celebrations. As the snow falls and Christmas Eve descends upon the town each year, anticipation mingles with the festive cheer. The town square fills with people, huddled together, their breath forming icy clouds in the crisp air. The clock ticks towards midnight, and then, with the ethereal chime of the hour, it begins - the soft, haunting strains of a spectral carol, drifting through the snow-laden air, a poignant serenade from the Caroling Specters of New England.

This Yuletide tale, steeped in history and woven with the spectral threads of the paranormal, reminds us of the interplay between joy and sorrow, life and death, the known and the unknown. As the final notes of the ghostly carol fade into the silent night, one can't help but feel an eerie sense of connection with the past, a spectral bond forged in the timeless spirit of Christmas.

The Yuletide Banshee in Irish Countryside

The merriment of the Yuletide season carries a haunting refrain in the Irish countryside, where ancient folklore and spectral encounters intertwine to weave a chilling Christmas tale. Welcome to the eerie narrative of the Yuletide Banshee.

Our tale unfolds in the quaint Irish hamlet of Ballygally. Nestled among rolling emerald hills and bordered by the wild North Atlantic, Ballygally is a picture of idyllic rural Ireland. Its charming thatched-roof cottages and warm-hearted inhabitants make it an inviting destination for Yuletide festivities. Yet, as the villagers prepare to celebrate the joyous holiday, a chilling harbinger of folklore looms over their merriment.

For as long as the elders of Ballygally can remember, each Christmas has been accompanied by an eerie phenomenon. As the last vestiges of daylight succumb to the winter night on

Christmas Eve, a mournful wail echoes through the hills. This is no ordinary cry but the haunting lament of the Banshee, a spectral figure deeply embedded in Irish mythology.

This Yuletide Banshee, as she has been christened, doesn't adhere to the traditional depiction of a banshee predicting death. Instead, her wails, as chilling as the winter wind, have become an ethereal part of Ballygally's Christmas celebrations. It's said that at the stroke of midnight, the air grows unnaturally cold, and then her keen echoes through the valleys, casting an eerie pallor over the Christmas festivities.

The first recorded account of this spectral Christmas guest dates back to 1872, when postmaster Patrick O'Shaughnessy documented his chilling encounter. In his account, he writes of the deafening silence that fell upon the hamlet as midnight approached on Christmas Eve. Then, as if carried by the wind, a mournful wail permeated the night. O'Shaughnessy describes the sound as the saddest melody he'd ever heard, filled with such sorrow that it moved him to tears.

In the generations since O'Shaughnessy's time, many Ballygally inhabitants and Yuletide visitors have reported encounters with the spectral banshee. Tales describe a misty figure, ethereal in the moonlit night, her long white hair seeming to merge with the winter snow. Eyewitness accounts speak of a profound sadness that accompanies her appearance, a sorrow that lingers in the air long after her wails have faded.

An eerie fascination with the Yuletide Banshee led local historians to delve into Ballygally's past. Their research led them to a tragic event in the winter of 1737, when a young woman named Aislinn disappeared in the hills on Christmas Eve. Despite extensive searches, she was never found, and the town grieved her assumed death. Over time, historians have speculated that Aislinn's restless spirit is the Yuletide Banshee, her sorrow echoing through the centuries.

Today, the wails of the Yuletide Banshee are an intrinsic part of Ballygally's Christmas traditions. As Christmas Eve descends upon the village, and homes are filled with warmth and merriment, the villagers gather around their hearths, exchanging stories of Aislinn and waiting for the haunting cry of the Banshee.

There's a poignant beauty in this spectral Christmas tradition, a reminder that amidst the joy of Yuletide, there are echoes of loss and longing. The Yuletide Banshee's wails, chilling as they are, add a depth to Ballygally's Christmas celebrations that transcends the temporal and connects the villagers with their spectral folklore.

So, dear reader, as you venture through these tales of haunted Christmases, spare a thought for Ballygally's Yuletide Banshee. Each Christmas Eve, as her haunting wails echo through the Irish countryside, they weave a spectral thread through the joyous tapestry of Yuletide, creating a chilling melody that resonates with the spirit of the season.

The Phantom Sleigh Bells of Siberia

The icy expanse of Siberia, a realm where nature reigns supreme and humans are mere transient visitors, is the setting of our next spectral Yuletide tale. Allow me to lead you through the blizzard swept wilderness and into the echoing mystery of the Phantom Sleigh Bells of Siberia.

Siberia, with its endless tundra and relentless winters, might not be the first location one associates with the merriment of Christmas. However, the resilient inhabitants of this austere region have fostered their unique Yuletide traditions. One such tradition is both a chilling mystery and an anticipated part of their Christmas celebrations: the sound of phantom sleigh bells echoing through the silent, snow-covered nights.

This spectral sound, as ethereal as the Northern Lights that often dance in the Siberian sky, first emerged in local anecdotes and legends in the 19th century. On Christmas Eve, as the Arctic cold descends upon the Siberian landscape and families huddle in their homes, a distant jingling breaks the silence. The sound, as many accounts describe, resembles the ringing of sleigh bells, growing louder as though approaching, then fading into the icy wilderness.

The first documented account of this phenomenon dates back to 1847, recorded by a fur trapper named Grigori Ivanovich. In his journal, he describes the night as unusually quiet, the snow falling softly onto the frozen ground. Then, from the desolate expanse, the jingling of sleigh bells began to echo. Ivanovich writes of his initial confusion, turning into fear as he realised the sound had no discernible source. The bells continued for several minutes before fading away as mysteriously as they had begun.

Over the years, numerous other accounts from villagers, explorers, and even scientists stationed in Siberia have added to the lore of the Phantom Sleigh Bells. Eyewitnesses often mention a sudden drop in temperature, a sense of unease, and occasionally a fleeting glimpse of a spectral figure driving a phantom sleigh across the snowy tundra.

Local legends speculate on the origin of this haunting Yuletide sound. One such tale speaks of an old Siberian herder named Nikolai, who would traverse the vast tundra every Christmas Eve to deliver gifts to the scattered communities. One fateful Christmas, a blizzard swept across the region, and Nikolai never returned. It is said that the phantom sleigh bells are Nikolai's spirit continuing his Yuletide journey, his dedication echoing through the Siberian wilderness.

Today, the eerie jingling of the Phantom Sleigh Bells has become an integral part of Siberian Christmas folklore. As families gather around their fires on Christmas Eve, they listen intently for the spectral chimes that signal the start of Yuletide.

This tale, steeped in the ethereal mystery of the Siberian wilderness, encapsulates the resilience of the human spirit. Despite the harsh conditions, the Siberian inhabitants have woven a spectral tale into their Christmas traditions, a tale that binds their communities and provides a spine-tingling twist to their Yuletide celebrations.

So, dear reader, as you journey through these eerie Yuletide tales from the world's most mystical corners, remember the sound of the Phantom Sleigh Bells. Let their spectral chimes remind you of the interconnectedness of joy and sorrow, the seen and unseen, and the living and the spectral that adds depth to our human experience. The Phantom Sleigh Bells of Siberia, a spectral sound in the vast wilderness, is a Yuletide reminder of the enduring spirit of humanity and the chilling beauty of our world's mysteries.

Santa's Spectral Visit in Melbourne

In the southern hemisphere, where the warmth of summer embraces Christmas celebrations, there exists a chilling tale that contrasts with the sunny Australian Yuletide. Allow me to transport you to Melbourne, where a spectral guest has been known to make a Christmas Eve appearance. Here, we recount the curious case of Santa's Spectral Visit.

Melbourne, the cultural hub of Australia, basks in its summer sun as December descends, creating a unique Christmas atmosphere. The streets hum with festive cheer, and homes shimmer with decorative lights that brighten the long, warm evenings. However, as Christmas Eve descends and families gather in celebration, one Melbourne household braces itself for a visit from a ghostly yuletide figure.

Our tale begins with the Hargreaves family, who reside in an ornate Victorian-era house in the suburb of Williamstown. For generations, the Hargreaves have reported an eerie visitor on Christmas Eve – a spectral Santa Claus.

The first recorded encounter dates back to 1903 when patriarch George Hargreaves documented his otherworldly experience. As the clock struck midnight, marking the arrival of Christmas Day, he was drawn to a strange glow emanating from the living room. As he approached, he was met with the sight of a ghostly figure, glowing in the dim light. The figure, donning a Santa Claus attire, was seen standing near the Christmas tree before it slowly faded away.

Over the years, many Hargreaves descendants and their Christmas guests have reported similar encounters. The spectral Santa is always described similarly: an ethereal glow, a traditional red suit, a long white beard, and an old-world charm. Eyewitnesses speak of an inexplicable calmness that fills the room, a sense of peace and goodwill that one associates with the spirit of Christmas.

The spectral Santa doesn't interact with the living, nor does he leave physical presents under the tree. His gift, it seems, is his presence itself – a spectral reminder of the joy, generosity, and goodwill that embody the Christmas spirit.

Local historians, intrigued by these accounts, began delving into the property's history. They discovered that the house was initially built and owned by a wealthy businessman, Thomas Sutherland, who was known for his Santa Claus impersonations at local Christmas gatherings. His charitable nature made him a beloved figure in the community. Unfortunately, Sutherland died in 1878, on a Christmas Eve, in his beloved home.

Many believe the spectral Santa is none other than Sutherland, continuing his Yuletide tradition from beyond the grave. His spirit, carrying the essence of Christmas, is thought to return to his former home each year, spreading festive cheer in his unique, spectral way.

Today, the anticipation of Santa's spectral visit has become an integral part of the Hargreaves family's Christmas celebrations. As the hours of Christmas Eve wind down, the family gathers in the living room, the air heavy with expectation. When the clock strikes midnight, the soft glow usually begins to form, and for a few hushed moments, the spectral Santa appears, bringing with him a profound sense of peace and joy.

This eerie Yuletide tale from Melbourne reminds us of the unique ways in which the spirit of Christmas touches us. In a world often driven by materialism, the Hargreaves' spectral Santa symbolises the immaterial and timeless essence of Christmas – peace, goodwill, and generosity. Even in his spectral form, he embodies the power of these values to transcend the physical realm, and touch hearts.

So, dear reader, as you traverse this collection of haunted Yuletide tales, remember the story of Santa's spectral visit. Amid the Christmas lights of sunny Melbourne, a ghostly figure in a Santa suit weaves a tale of Yuletide cheer that echoes from the spectral realm into the hearts of the living. It is a haunting yet heartwarming reminder of the eternal spirit of Christmas that continues to bring joy and warmth to our lives, even from beyond the grave.

The Christmas Eve Poltergeist of Prague

As we continue our journey through the world's most haunted Christmas traditions, let's step into the heart of Central Europe. Nestled amidst the cobblestone streets and the Gothic architecture of Prague lies a tale that blends festive cheer with unsettling occurrences. Here, we recount the eerie story of the Christmas Eve Poltergeist of Prague.

The magical city of Prague, with its iconic Prague Castle and the famous Charles Bridge, takes on a uniquely enchanting aura during Christmas. As the scent of Trdelník, traditional Czech pastries, fills the air, and the festive markets at Old Town Square bustle with cheerful crowds, an imposing Baroque mansion in Mala Strana, aptly named 'the House of the Black Madonna,' cloaks a chilling tale.

For several generations, the Kovařovic family have resided in this mansion. The Kovařovics, known for their hospitality, often opened their doors to family, friends, and neighbours for a grand Christmas Eve dinner. However, a guest of a more ethereal nature seemed to have taken a liking to these yuletide gatherings.

As family folklore goes, every Christmas Eve, as the Kovařovics indulged in their festive celebrations, strange happenings began to occur. It started subtly: the sound of footsteps echoing in the empty hallways, the chandeliers swinging gently with no breeze, the flickering of lights. But as the night progressed, the phenomena escalated.

Doors would slam shut, cutlery would rattle in their drawers, and Christmas decorations would levitate before dropping to the ground. The grand piano in the drawing-room would play disjointed melodies, and cold gusts of wind would sweep through the rooms, despite all windows and doors being tightly shut.

Over the years, numerous eyewitnesses confirmed these baffling incidents. Guests, many initially sceptical, would leave with a shiver down their spines and a story they could scarcely believe. Despite the unsettling happenings, no one ever reported feeling threatened. The spectral presence, though mischievous, seemed more interested in participating in the festivities than causing harm.

Intriguingly, these disturbances would cease at the stroke of midnight, with the tolling of the bell from the nearby St. Nicholas Church. The family would then gather around the Christmas tree to exchange gifts, the earlier incidents casting an eerie memory on their joyful tradition.

Fascinated and perturbed by these annual occurrences, the Kovařovics sought the help of local paranormal investigators. The investigators, after spending a few eventful Christmas Eves at the mansion, concluded that the activities were consistent with those typically attributed to a poltergeist, a type of ghost known for its ability to manipulate the physical environment.

The history of the house offered a potential explanation. The House of the Black Madonna, before becoming the Kovařovic family's residence, was a local tavern during the 18th century. It was known for its Christmas Eve gatherings, much loved by Prague's townsfolk.

One of its regular patrons was a man named Ondřej, known for his love of the Yuletide season. As the tale goes, Ondřej died tragically on a Christmas Eve when, on his way to the tavern, he fell into the icy Vltava River. Many believe that it is his spirit, still eager to partake in the Christmas Eve revelry, that returns to the house each year.

The tale of the Christmas Eve Poltergeist of Prague is a chilling reminder that the veil between our world and the spectral realm might thin during significant occasions. As the Kovařovics and their guests gather for their annual Christmas Eve dinner, they also prepare for their uninvited guest. The flickering lights, the moving objects, and the eerie music serve not only as spine-chilling entertainment but also as a testament to the eternal reach of the Christmas spirit.

For Ondřej, his love for Christmas transcended the barriers of life and death. His spectral presence is a spectral note of festive cheer, a reminder of the shared love for the Yuletide season that connects the living, the dead, and the eternal city of Prague.

As an investigator of the paranormal, tales such as these serve as a poignant reminder that even in the most chilling encounters, there is often a thread of humanity. It's a lesson to cherish our traditions, our connections, and our shared love for Christmas.

After all, we never know how long its influence may last, perhaps even beyond the realm of the living.

The Cursed Christmas Market of Bavaria

As we continue our eerie exploration of haunted Christmas tales from around the globe, we venture into the snowy landscapes of Germany, specifically, to the festive region of Bavaria. This corner of the world, renowned for its enchanting Christmas markets, hides a spooky secret. It is the home of a particularly cursed Christmas market, a place where the joyous celebrations of the season intertwine with unexplainable phenomena.

Welcome to the infamous Weihnachtsmarkt, or Christmas market, of Oberammergau, a quaint village known for its ornate wood carvings, striking frescoes, and a haunting tale that has intrigued paranormal enthusiasts for decades.

The Oberammergau Weihnachtsmarkt, held in the village square surrounded by the Bavarian Alps, boasts an array of traditional handicrafts, mouth-watering delicacies, and a uniquely eerie phenomenon that adds a chilling edge to the otherwise cheerful festivities.

It was in the winter of 1956 when the first accounts of peculiar occurrences began to emerge. Market goers spoke of an unseen force that seemed to breathe an icy chill down their necks, a fleeting touch when no one was near, and a sense of unease that lingered like the winter fog.

As the years passed, these sensations were accompanied by an apparition. Many claimed to see a figure, a woman, dressed in traditional Bavarian clothing, wandering amidst the market stalls. The spectral figure, described as having an ethereal glow, would wander the market, pausing occasionally to admire the goods, and then vanish into the cold night.

A particular stall seemed to be the centre of this spectral activity. Helmut Schneider, a local woodcarver, and his booth of intricately carved Nativity figures were the seeming favourite of this ghostly visitor. He shared his first encounter with this apparition in the winter of 1971.

"I was packing up for the day, and out of the corner of my eye, I saw a woman looking at my figures," Helmut recalled. "Thinking it was a late customer, I approached her, but as I did, she vanished. It startled me, but I didn't feel threatened."

This spectral woman's appearance became an annual event, adding a dash of the uncanny to the festive air. Though many felt a chill run down their spines upon seeing her, none reported feeling threatened.

Intrigued by this persistent haunting, I travelled to Oberammergau in December of 2022 to experience this phenomenon first-hand. There, I met Elsa Schmidt, a longtime resident and a historian, who offered a possible explanation for these hauntings.

According to local lore, the ghost is believed to be that of Frieda Bauer, a resident of Oberammergau in the early 19th century. Frieda was known for her love of the Christmas season and the local Weihnachtsmarkt, where she sold her homemade gingerbread. Tragically, Frieda met an untimely death when she got lost in a blizzard returning from the market. It is her spirit that locals believe returns to her favourite place every year.

I spent a few nights in the market, amidst the twinkling lights and the wafting aroma of Glühwein and roasted chestnuts, waiting for Frieda to make her appearance. And true to the accounts, on a particularly cold night, I saw her. A faint figure in traditional clothing, appearing and disappearing among the crowd, her ethereal presence adding an otherworldly charm to the festive market.

The story of the cursed Christmas market of Bavaria serves as a chilling reminder of the thin veil separating the world of the living and the dead. Even in death, Frieda's spirit is drawn to the joyous energy of the Christmas market.

This spectral tale doesn't detract from the merriment of the season; instead, it adds a layer of mystery, a peculiar tradition unique to the Oberammergau Weihnachtsmarkt. It serves as a reminder that our love for the Yuletide season can linger on, perhaps even beyond the grave.

As an investigator of the paranormal, I believe in the unseen, the unexplained, and the mysterious, just as much as I believe in the magic of Christmas. The tale of Frieda and the haunted Christmas market of Bavaria is a testament to this belief. The mingling of the supernatural with the festivities is a unique way of celebrating the holiday spirit, a peculiar tradition that keeps the memory of Frieda alive.

So, next time you find yourself wandering through a Christmas market, keep an eye out for the unexpected. For you never know when you might encounter the spectral side of Christmas, a reminder of the eternal spirit of Yuletide celebrations that can transcend the boundaries of life and death.

The Lost Carolers of Canterbury

In the heart of England, nestled amidst the idyllic Kent countryside, lies the historical city of Canterbury. Rich in heritage, and teeming with tales of a bygone era, this city is also the setting for a hauntingly beautiful Christmas mystery - The Lost Carolers of Canterbury.

Known for its magnificent cathedral and the site of pilgrimage in Chaucer's legendary tales, Canterbury holds a special place in the yuletide folklore of England. Every Christmas Eve, as the city dons its festive charm, the cobblestoned streets echo with a melody that transcends the barriers of time. The dulcet tones of traditional carols sung by spectral figures fill the air, enchanting and mystifying in equal measure.

The tale of the lost carolers dates back to the Great War, a time when the world was cloaked in the shadows of despair. The war had taken away many a father, son, and brother, leaving behind families to celebrate the joyous season with heavy hearts. Yet, despite their loss, the people of Canterbury found solace in unity, coming together to continue their cherished tradition of carolling.

One particular group, a choir of seven men, held the community together with their uplifting melodies. Known for their exceptional harmonies, they would journey through the city streets every Christmas Eve, spreading cheer with their songs. However, in December 1916, a tragedy struck that would forever change the fabric of this beloved tradition.

The choir set out to sing, as they had every year, wrapped in warm coats to fend off the biting winter chill. As the night grew darker, a heavy snowstorm engulfed the city. The choir, undeterred by the weather, continued their carolling, their voices ringing out against the howling wind. But as the storm worsened, they disappeared into the white abyss, never to be seen again.

The loss of the choir was deeply felt by the residents, their absence a stark reminder of the war's far-reaching effects. But when the next Christmas Eve rolled around, something strange occurred. As midnight approached, the familiar harmonies of carols filled the silent night. People who dared to venture out saw the shadowy figures of seven men, singing their hearts out, undeterred by the physical world's constraints.

I was drawn to this story by its unique blend of Christmas tradition and supernatural occurrence. In December 2022, I decided to spend Christmas Eve in Canterbury to witness this phenomenon for myself. I was not disappointed. As the clock struck midnight, I heard the melodic notes of 'Hark! The Herald Angels Sing' wafting through the crisp winter air. I followed the sound until I arrived at a dimly lit alleyway.

There, I saw them. Seven figures, semi-transparent and glowing faintly, stood in a tight circle, singing with an intensity that defied their spectral form. The notes of their song hung in the cold air, their ethereal voices weaving a captivating harmony. I stood there, mesmerised by the sight, the carols resounding in the silent, snow-covered city.

Later, I spoke to local historian, Judith Archer, who has been studying the tale of the lost carolers for years. She believes that the spectral choir is the very same group of men lost in the snowstorm. "They're holding onto the tradition they loved, continuing to spread the Christmas spirit even from the other side," she explained.

The tale of the Lost Carolers of Canterbury is a haunting yet heartwarming reminder of the enduring spirit of Christmas, a testament to the power of tradition, unity, and the unyielding joy of the festive season. Their spectral carols serve as an annual tribute to those lost during the war, their voices a melodic echo from the past that continues to fill the Canterbury streets with a haunting Christmas melody. The sight and sound of them are a Christmas gift, a moment of enchanting, eerie wonder in an otherwise ordinary world. And while their tale is shrouded in sorrow, their continued presence is a testament to the enduring magic of Christmas, a melody of hope in the heart of winter.

The Yule Lads' Haunting of Icelandic Winters

Iceland, a land of fire and ice, a place where nature is raw, and the elements can be as harsh as they are beautiful. This Nordic island, tucked away near the Arctic circle, has a rich tapestry of folklore woven into its culture, and the Christmas season is no exception. Today, I share with you the chilling tale of the Yule Lads, thirteen mischievous spirits of Icelandic folklore, who, during the Yuletide season, are believed to come down from the mountains to play tricks on the inhabitants of this frosty wonderland.

For thirteen nights leading up to Christmas, Icelandic children place their best shoes by the window, hoping to wake up to treats left by the Yule Lads. If they have been well-behaved, they are rewarded with gifts. But those who misbehave find only a rotten potato in their shoe, a stern reminder of the thirteen spectral figures watching their actions.

Each of the Yule Lads has a unique character, reflected in their names and their peculiar habits. There's Stekkjarstaur, or Sheep-Cote Clod, who harasses the sheep but is impaired by his stiff peg-legs. Pottaskefill, or Pot Scraper, steals leftovers from pots, while Askasleikir, or Bowl Licker, hides under beds waiting to steal bowls of food. From Door Slammer, who makes noise at night by slamming doors, to Window Peeper, who gazes into windows in search of things to steal, each of these lads is a unique troublemaker in their own right.

Now, while this might seem like an unusual and somewhat eerie Christmas tradition to outsiders, the Icelanders accept it as a part of their Yuletide celebrations. However, in recent years, the tale of the Yule Lads has taken a more chilling turn. There have been numerous accounts of encounters with these spectral pranksters that lend an even more supernatural tone to the folklore.

In the winter of 2022, I found myself in the picturesque town of Akureyri, hoping to delve deeper into the mysterious Yule Lad sightings. I met with a local family, the Jónssons, who shared a fascinating account of their encounter with the Yule Lads. The patriarch, Magnus, a fisherman by trade and a storyteller at heart, recalled an incident from a few winters ago.

It was a week before Christmas, and the Jónssons were settling in for the night, the children eagerly placing their shoes by the window before climbing into their beds. In the dead of night, Magnus was awakened by a ruckus downstairs. Assuming it to be the wind, he tried to go back to sleep but the noise persisted. Cautiously, he went to investigate and was taken aback by the sight that met his eyes.

In his own words, "There they were, huddled together, bickering, and rummaging through our pantry. Thirteen figures, more shadowy than solid, causing a right old mess. One was licking our bowls clean, another slamming the doors, while one peeked through our window into the stormy night. I stood frozen, watching them, their ghostly forms semi-transparent in the dim light."

Magnus shared his experience with his neighbours the next day and discovered they too had similar encounters. The Yule Lads, it seemed, were no longer just figures of folklore but had transcended into a more spectral form, their antics casting an eerie glow on the festive season.

These experiences, while unsettling, have become a part of the local lore, adding a dash of supernatural intrigue to Iceland's unique Yuletide celebrations. The Yule Lads' haunting serves as an annual reminder of the country's rich folklore, its tales spun around the fireside on cold winter nights. And even though the spectral visits of the Yule Lads may leave a chill in the air, the Icelandic people embrace these tales, for they believe that the Yule Lads, in their own mischievous way, embody the spirit of Christmas - a season of storytelling, of magic, and of a little bit of mischief.

As I wrap up this tale, tucked away in the warmth of an Akureyri inn, while a winter storm rages outside, I can't help but glance at the window. A pair of well-worn boots sit there, hopeful for gifts come morning. But as the wind howls and the snowflakes swirl, I can't shake off the feeling that somewhere out there in the white expanse, thirteen spectral figures are watching, waiting for the chance to engage in their Yuletide tricks. And perhaps, just perhaps, that's what makes an Icelandic Christmas all the more magical, all the more mysterious, and all the more haunted.

The Bewitched Christmas Tree of Nova Scotia

Nova Scotia, Canada, a province known for its scenic beauty, high tides, and welcoming communities. It's also home to the most extraordinary Christmas tradition – providing Boston, USA, with a grand Christmas tree each year as a thank you for their assistance after the devastating Halifax Explosion of 1917. But today, I take you to a small town in this maritime province where a different Christmas tree takes centre stage, not for its grandeur or radiance, but for its paranormal peculiarity. This is the tale of the Bewitched Christmas Tree of Nova Scotia.

Our story starts in the quaint town of Lunenburg, a UNESCO World Heritage Site known for its vibrant architecture and a history rooted deeply in maritime tradition. It's here, in a centuries-old home, that the eccentric phenomenon takes place.

The MacDonald family has lived in this home for generations.

Their home is like many others in town - a charming, colourful 'Lunenburg Bump' style house - except for one peculiarity. Every Christmas, they put up their traditional family Christmas tree, an old faux pine passed down the generations, decorated with an array of vintage and handcrafted ornaments. But according to the MacDonalds, this isn't an ordinary Christmas tree; it reportedly moves on its own accord every Christmas.

I visited Lunenburg in December 2019 to meet the MacDonald family and to witness this curious event firsthand. Dora MacDonald, a vivacious woman in her seventies, was my host. She welcomed me into her warm home, a stark contrast to the freezing Atlantic wind howling outside.

"The tree's been with us for as long as I can remember," Dora told me as we sipped hot cocoa by the fire, "My mother got it from her mother, who got it from her mother, and so on. It's an heirloom, but with a bit of a twist."

According to Dora, every Christmas, the tree displays a peculiar habit of moving around. "Not too much, you understand," she said, "It's not as if it's dancing a jig. But we'd leave it in one spot, and the next morning, it would have moved a few inches to a foot. Nothing much, but enough to notice."

I asked if they had found any logical explanation – a slant in the floor, perhaps, or a prank-playing family member. But Dora dismissed these with a shake of her head. "The floor's as level as a field, and we've all seen it move, even when we're alone in the house. Besides," she added, her eyes twinkling, "it only happens during the Christmas season. Once we pack it away on Epiphany, it stays put till next December."

The MacDonalds' account was fascinating, and I was eager to observe this bewitched tree. Over the next few days, I spent time with the family, participating in their Yuletide celebrations, and watching the tree. True to Dora's word, the tree moved slightly each night, its new position noticeable each morning. On one notable night, I awoke to a rustling sound and caught the tree shifting, the ornaments clinking softly.

After several nights of observations and countless hours of footage, it was evident the phenomenon wasn't a hoax. The movement was subtle and, I admit, not overly dramatic, but it was unexplainable. A paranormal investigator by profession, I've encountered numerous cases of objects moving seemingly on their own. But the Bewitched Christmas Tree of Nova Scotia was different. It was unique in that the activity was contained to a specific time of year, and despite its ghostly behaviour, it didn't instil fear. Instead, it added a sense of otherworldly wonder to the family's Christmas celebration.

As I left Lunenburg, the MacDonald family waved me off from their porch, their bewitched Christmas tree twinkling merrily behind the window. Their story, in all its supernatural charm, was a testament to the magic and mystery that Christmas brings. The Bewitched Christmas Tree of Nova Scotia was a delightful enigma, a spectral touch to the festive season that the McDonalds had come to love and anticipate.

As we delve into the world of Yuletide mysteries and unearth tales that make us question the world as we know it, we learn that not all paranormal phenomena are ominous. Some, like the McDonalds' Christmas tree, are an enchanting blend of the mysterious and the festive, adding a dash of spectral charm to the most wonderful time of the year.

The Disappearing Ornaments of Oslo

Oslo, the capital of Norway, a city known for its rich history, magnificent fjords, and vibrant Christmas celebrations. But amidst the joyful Yuletide festivities, there lies a tale that is sure to give even the most ardent Christmas lover a chill. This is the story of the Disappearing Ornaments of Oslo, a tale that unfolds within the historic confines of a stately mansion in Oslo's distinguished Frogner district.

The mansion, a grand display of 19th-century neoclassical architecture, stands majestically, seemingly unperturbed by the passage of time. Its current occupants, the Bjørnstad family, are descendants of a long line of sea merchants who have called this mansion home for generations. But it is during Christmas, as lights twinkle, and the mansion dons a festive look, that the inexplicable events unfold.

Each Christmas, the Bjørnstad family adorns a towering Norwegian spruce with ornaments that are as old as the mansion itself. These heirloom ornaments are exquisitely handcrafted, some of them dating back several centuries. But over the years, the family noticed a peculiar occurrence - the ornaments would inexplicably disappear, only to reappear in the most unusual places.

Ingeborg Bjørnstad, the matriarch of the family, first noticed this uncanny event when she was a young girl. The family would wake up to find ornaments missing from the tree, only to discover them later, often in places that were out of reach or hardly frequented. One ornament turned up inside a sealed attic trunk, another was found nestled in the pages of a book in the vast library, while yet another was discovered in the mansion's ancient root cellar.

This mysterious tradition continued, with the ornaments vanishing and reappearing every Christmas, much to the bewilderment of the Bjørnstad family. Attempts to explain these events logically proved futile. The mansion was secure, and there were no signs of intruders. The family themselves had no reason or motive to orchestrate such an elaborate and prolonged prank. Plus, the phenomenon had been occurring for so long that it spanned multiple generations of Bjørnstads.

But the peculiarity of the vanishing ornaments didn't stop at their strange relocations. Some family members and guests claimed to see the ornaments moving on their own. They reported seeing a soft glow around an ornament before it vanished right before their eyes. Others noticed a faint hum or a whispering sound just as an ornament disappeared.

Despite these eerie events, there was no sense of malice or threat associated with the phenomenon. Instead, it seemed to instil a sense of festive wonder and anticipation, albeit of a more spectral kind. The family eagerly awaited the annual "trip" of the ornaments, and each discovery became a part of their unique Christmas celebrations. Guests were regaled with tales of the Disappearing Ornaments of Oslo, and those fortunate enough to witness an ornament's disappearance were considered part of the mansion's rich Yuletide lore.

As the story of the Bjørnstad's Christmas mystery spread, paranormal enthusiasts and investigators tried to unravel this curious case. They conducted numerous studies and vigils, especially around Christmas, hoping to catch the ornaments in action. Despite capturing some unexplainable movements and faint auras on camera, the mystery remains unsolved.

So, the tale of the Disappearing Ornaments of Oslo continues, woven into the festive fabric of the city, a testament to the spectral enchantment of Christmas. The Bjørnstad family's unusual Yuletide tradition reminds us that while Christmas is a time of joy, love, and unity, it can also hold a touch of the inexplicable, a hint of the supernatural. It serves to show that, perhaps, the world is not as we always perceive it to be and that the realm of the paranormal might be more intertwined with our own than we think.

And so, as the snow falls gently on the streets of Oslo, and the city lights up in celebration of Christmas, the grand mansion in Frogner stands resolute, harbouring its age-old secret. Inside, the Norwegian spruce stands tall and proud, adorned with its ancient ornaments that might just disappear and then reappear in the most unexpected places. And therein lies the magic and mystery of the Disappearing Ornaments of Oslo - a tale that, while shrouded in the supernatural, is ultimately an affirmation of the wondrous and unpredictable spirit of Christmas.

The Christmas Goblin of Greece

This chapter opens against the backdrop of a quaint, rustic village in the heart of Greece. Kallikrateia, with its whitewashed houses and cobbled streets, overlooks the cerulean waters of the Aegean Sea. The villagers, known for their deep-seated belief in the old ways and traditions, cherish the festive period of Christmas with an intensity that rivals their fervour for mythology. And it is during this time that the eerie tale of the Christmas Goblin, known locally as the 'kallikantzari', unfolds.

The kallikantzari are creatures steeped in Greek folklore. They are said to dwell underground and spend their time sawing away at the 'World Tree', a colossal tree that supports the Earth. But when Christmas approaches, they ascend to the surface and run amok, spreading mischief and chaos wherever they tread.

These goblins are believed to surface from their subterranean dwellings on Christmas day and remain topside until Epiphany, the 6th of January, wreaking havoc during this Twelve Days of Christmas. They sneak into homes through any available crevices, chasms, or doorways, bringing along their potent aura of disorder.

Among the villagers, a particular family, the Papadopoulos, have been living in Kallikrateia for countless generations. They, like their ancestors before them, have been keepers of this tale, and some say, the unwitting hosts to these annual, unwanted Christmas guests.

It was Christmas Eve, and as was tradition, the family was making preparations to keep the kallikantzari at bay. The hearth was kept burning day and night as the goblins were believed to detest light and fire. The house was smudged with basil, thought to repel these creatures, and a large wooden cross, blackened by the Christmas hearth's flame, was hung at the front door.

Despite their best efforts, peculiar incidents started occurring from Christmas Day onwards. The food meant for Christmas feasting was found scattered in the kitchen, their beloved pet cat was found hiding in fright under the couch, unusual scratches appeared on wooden surfaces, and strange sounds echoed through their house at night. The air in the house grew heavy, and an inexplicable chill ran down their spine every so often.

Yiannis Papadopoulos, the head of the family, recalled an especially eerie incident. He was awakened in the middle of the night by the sound of laughter – a sinister, guttural chuckle that sent waves of dread coursing through him. He stepped out of his bed and moved towards the sound. As he entered the living room, he saw the Christmas tree shaking violently, its ornaments jingling in discord. He felt a gust of wind sweep past him, and the front door flung open, the laughter receding into the dark, cold night.

These unusual incidents were not confined to the Papadopoulos household alone. Other villagers too reported strange occurrences – food and possessions disturbed, bizarre noises, fleeting shadows, the unease of being watched, and the constant feeling of mischief afoot.

However, come Epiphany, the strange occurrences ceased as abruptly as they had started. The villagers drew a collective sigh of relief. The priest, in the age-old custom, went from house to house, sprinkling holy water, signifying the cleansing of their homes from the Christmas goblins' influence and marking the end of their 12-day mischief.

The tale of the Christmas Goblin of Greece is not merely a spooky account of holiday hauntings. It is interwoven into the region's festive fabric, adding an element of tantalising fright to the otherwise cheerful Yuletide celebrations. The villagers of Kallikrateia, like their ancestors, have passed down these tales of the kallikantzari, imprinting a part of their cultural and mythological heritage onto the Christmas festivities.

As the Christmas lights twinkle in the quiet village of Kallikrateia, one can almost imagine the mischief-laden cackles of the goblins echoing through the chilly night air, reminding us that Christmas, in all its warmth and joy, carries a touch of the eerie, the mystical, and the uncanny. After all, when the veil between worlds is believed to be the thinnest, who can say what might come visiting? And therein lies the haunting charm of the Christmas Goblin of Greece. A charm that, while shrouded in the supernatural, brings an undeniable richness to the tapestry of Yuletide folklore, revealing that the spirit of Christmas can sometimes be just as thrilling as it is jolly.

The Ghostly Procession in Colonial Williamsburg

In the heart of Virginia, in the United States, nestled along the James River, sits the historic city of Williamsburg. Known for its crucial role in America's early history, Williamsburg is a city that does not forget its past. This becomes especially apparent when the Christmas season arrives, and the old cobblestone streets, colonial buildings, and festive decorations transport one back to a bygone era. Among the age-old traditions and the joyous festivities, an unusual tale reverberates—one that blurs the line between the living and the dead, the real and the spectral.

Williamsburg, once the capital of the Colony of Virginia, is a city steeped in history. It's no surprise then that this historic city is believed to be home to several ghostly inhabitants. But the story that stands out during the Christmas season revolves around the spectres seen on the city's historic thoroughfare, the Duke of Gloucester Street.

It begins as a quiet whisper on the breeze on Christmas Eve—a faint rhythm of a drum. The residents and visitors who have experienced this phenomenon recall that as the night descends, the drum's rhythm becomes louder, transforming from a distant echo into a haunting tattoo. A chill descends over the area, causing shivers despite the winter coats and layers of warm clothing.

Then, as the clock strikes midnight, a spectral procession reportedly appears. Witnesses claim that a ghostly group of colonial soldiers starts marching down the Duke of Gloucester Street, their transparent figures glowing in the moonlight. The soldiers, clad in colonial-era uniforms, their muskets gleaming, are seen to keep time to the eerie beat of the drum. Witnesses have noted the solemn determination on their translucent faces as they march in formation, seemingly unaware of the living world around them.

Lucy Hughes, a long-term resident of Williamsburg, recounts her experience. "It was Christmas Eve, a few years back. I was walking home after the midnight service. As I neared Duke of Gloucester Street, I heard the drum. Then I saw them—soldiers, marching in a formation. I couldn't believe my eyes. I could see the trees and buildings through them! They just marched down the street, then vanished as they reached the Capitol."

Visitors to the city have reported similar experiences, especially those staying in the colonial houses along the Duke of Gloucester Street. They have spoken about hearing the drum's rhythmic beat and seeing the spectral procession march past their windows, their ghostly faces devoid of any acknowledgement of their surroundings.

Researchers and local historians believe that these spirits might be remnants of a colonial-era military regiment, possibly tied to the Revolutionary War. Their march seems to echo a timeless tribute, their spectral presence a reminder of a turbulent past.

Intriguingly, the phenomenon repeats itself each Christmas, with the ghostly drum's beat and the soldiers' spectral march becoming an integral part of the city's Yuletide lore. Many a brave heart now makes it a point to visit the Duke of Gloucester Street on Christmas Eve, hoping to witness this eerie spectacle.

"The Ghostly Procession in Colonial Williamsburg" stands as an eerie, spine-tingling tale in the midst of Yuletide cheer. The city's historic charm, coupled with this spectral legend, imbues Williamsburg's Christmas celebrations with an uncanny allure.

The marching spectres, in their silent vigil, serve as a stark reminder of the city's storied past—a past that continues to echo through its streets, in the rhythm of a ghostly drum, and the determined march of its spectral soldiers, undeterred by the passage of time, forever bound to their Christmas Eve procession.

This tale, while unsettling, adds an unexpected dimension to the festive season. It serves as a bridge between the living and the dead, the past and the present. And as the snow falls gently on Duke of Gloucester Street, one can almost hear the drumbeat in the wind, and see the ghostly figures in the swirling snowflakes—a haunting Yuletide tale that adds to the mystique of a Christmas in Williamsburg.

The Haunting Hum of Helsinki

As the Finnish winter wraps the city of Helsinki in a chilling embrace, the city's oldest buildings reverberate with an eerie tale. On the longest night of the year, as people seek warmth in companionship and the Yuletide spirit, an unsettling, inexplicable phenomenon occurs—a mysterious hum that fills the air, turning an otherwise merry Christmas night into an experience of spectral resonance.

Historic Helsinki, the capital of Finland, is a city that juxtaposes the old with the new. Its architectural heritage stands as silent testimony to its past, and it is within the walls of these old buildings that the haunting hum is said to originate.

The phenomenon, described by many as an uncanny, almost otherworldly hum, can only be heard on Christmas night. It begins just as the clock strikes midnight, marking the start of the traditional Finnish Christmas. It is said to emanate from the walls of the oldest buildings, their stone and brickwork vibrating with a sound that is as chilling as it is bewildering. The hum, while barely audible, is felt more than heard—a deep, resonating vibration that seems to echo in the very bones of those who experience it.

Eyewitness accounts of the haunting hum have accumulated over the years. One such account comes from Martti Jokinen, a long-time resident of Helsinki and the owner of a 19th-century building that stands near the city's historic Senate Square.

"I first noticed it years ago," Martti recalls. "I was hosting a Christmas party at my place, and just as the bells of the Helsinki Cathedral tolled midnight, I felt it. A strange, inexplicable hum that seemed to come from the walls themselves. At first, I thought it was the effect of the cold, but the hum continued. It was faint, almost elusive, but undeniably there."

The hum is not limited to one location. Numerous testimonies from across Helsinki—from Kruununhaka to Eira—report the same phenomenon. Buildings dating back to the 18th and 19th centuries seem to be the epicentres, their age-old walls holding an eerie secret that only reveals itself on Christmas night.

Over the years, many theories have emerged in an attempt to explain this mysterious occurrence. Some believe it to be a form of 'resonant frequency,' a result of weather changes specific to Christmas night. Others are convinced that it is the result of an underground river flowing beneath the city. However, none of these explanations account for the hum's peculiar timing—occurring only on Christmas night.

A more popular, albeit unsettling, theory embraces the paranormal. Many locals, and indeed visitors who have experienced the phenomenon, speak of a spectral energy associated with the city's history. They believe that the hum is an echo of the city's past—a ghostly reminder of times and lives gone by.

Among them is Laura Salo, a Helsinki native and amateur historian. She shares, "Helsinki has a rich and varied history. I like to think that the hum is the city speaking to us. It's telling us stories, whispering its past into our present. Why only on Christmas night, one may ask. Well, Christmas is a time of reflection, of family and memories. Perhaps it's the city's way of remembering its own."

While the source of the haunting hum remains a mystery, its

occurrence has become an eerie yet integral part of Christmas in Helsinki. Every Christmas night, as locals and tourists celebrate, the city adds its spectral voice to the Yuletide cheer. The haunting hum, resonating through the city's oldest structures, serves as a chilling reminder of Helsinki's history, its spectral whispers weaving a ghostly melody into the joyous cacophony of Christmas.

In the end, "The Haunting Hum of Helsinki" remains a spectral secret, cloaked in the chilling embrace of the Finnish winter. A mystery that adds to the city's charm, turning Christmas night in Helsinki into a uniquely haunting experience—an eerie Yuletide tale that dances on the edge of the surreal, where the sound of the past resonates in the present.

The Haunted Advent Calendar of Vienna

In the heart of Austria, nestled amidst the enchanting landscapes and historical grandeur, stands the city of Vienna. Known for its rich culture and architectural marvels, Vienna is a city that exudes a timeless charm. But as Christmas descends, casting its spell of joy and togetherness, a chilling tale unfolds within the hallowed corridors of an ancient Viennese home. This tale is centred around an advent calendar—an heirloom piece that has been in the possession of the Müller family for generations. A tale that intertwines the festive spirit of Christmas with eerie occurrences, providing an uncanny undertone to the Yuletide cheer.

The Muller residence, a baroque building nestled in the heart of the city, is where our story unfolds. The advent calendar, a beautifully crafted piece of antiquity with intricately carved figures and motifs, has been a part of their family's Christmas tradition for as long as anyone can remember. Every year, on the first day of December, the family gathers to mark the beginning of Advent by opening the first door on the calendar.

However, this is no ordinary Advent calendar. Every year, with the opening of each door, a series of inexplicable incidents occur, casting a haunting shadow over the family's Christmas festivities. From objects moving of their own accord, strange whispers echoing through the halls, to the chilling sensation of an unseen presence, the Müller household becomes a hotbed of eerie happenings.

Take, for instance, the account of Heinrich Müller, the current head of the family. A pragmatic man by nature, Heinrich was initially sceptical of the tales surrounding the advent calendar. However, his scepticism was replaced with bemused acceptance after a chilling encounter of his own.

"It was the seventh day of December," Heinrich recounts. "I had just opened the seventh door on the calendar, a tiny carving of an angel. Later that night, I was awakened by the sound of hushed whispers. I searched the house, but everyone was fast asleep. The whispers seemed to be coming from the living room. When I entered, I saw the calendar aglow with an otherworldly light, and the whispers... they turned into a choir of voices, singing a Christmas carol in a language I couldn't recognize."

Another account comes from Heinrich's daughter, Elsa. One December evening, after opening the door corresponding to the day's date, she claimed to have seen spectral figures reflected in the house's antique mirror. "They looked like people from another time," Elsa said. "They were dressed in clothing that looked centuries old, and they seemed to be... celebrating. There was music, laughter, and dancing. It was like looking into a Christmas party from the past."

Despite the chilling experiences, the family has never considered discarding the calendar. "It is part of our family history," says Heinrich. "Sure, it gives us a fright every year, but no harm has ever come of it. In its own strange way, it adds to our Christmas experience."

Indeed, the haunted Advent calendar of Vienna is a tale that brings a unique flavour to the city's Christmas lore. It encapsulates the spirit of Yuletide—a time when the veil between the past and the present seems to thin, and a sense of magic hangs in the air. The strange occurrences, while eerie, bind the Müller family closer, a testament to the unifying spirit of

Christmas.

Whether a bridge to Vienna's spectral past, or simply a manifestation of the city's Yuletide magic, the haunted Advent calendar stands as a captivating tale from the world's mystical corners. It serves as a reminder that even in the season of joy and giving, there are mysteries that elude understanding. And in the end, isn't that what makes Christmas truly enchanting?

As the city of Vienna wraps itself in the festive spirit, amidst the twinkling lights, Christmas carols, and falling snow, the Müller family readies itself for another advent season, with its beloved haunted calendar. A part of their tradition, their family, their Christmas. A tale that adds an eerie yet fascinating contour to the world's collection of Yuletide tales.

And so, the story of the haunted Advent calendar continues, adding a hint of the uncanny to Vienna's Christmas cheer, a spectral echo that resonates amidst the Yuletide celebrations. A story that reflects the paradox of Christmas—the joyous cheer intertwined with mystery, the familiar mingled with the unknown, creating a unique tapestry of festive folklore that transcends time and space. In this city, at this time of the year, one can truly sense the ethereal magic of a haunted Christmas.

The Shrouded Specter of Shanghai's Silent Night

In the bustling metropolis of Shanghai, amidst the towering skyscrapers and winding lanes, stands the city's oldest church, the Holy Trinity. A sanctuary of quiet reflection in the vibrant city, the Gothic Revival style building has been a witness to the city's transformations, its walls echoing with stories of its past. However, as Christmas approaches, and the church prepares to celebrate the birth of Christ, an enigmatic tale begins to unfold, one that has been whispered among the congregants for generations. It is the tale of a spectral figure, a shrouded spectre that is said to visit the church every Christmas Eve, known to the locals as the "Shrouded Specter of Shanghai's Silent Night."

As the story goes, as the clock strikes midnight on Christmas Eve, a figure shrouded in an ancient robe makes its solemn procession through the aisle of the Holy Trinity, its footsteps echoing in the silence of the night. While the figure itself remains indistinct, concealed by the robe, the presence is palpable, a spectral silhouette casting a haunting presence in the sacred hall. It is said that the figure walks up to the altar, kneeling in silent prayer before disappearing as mysteriously as it appeared. This spectral visitation has become a part of the church's Christmas tradition, the eerie tale adding a layer of intrigue to the festive cheer.

Many who have attended the midnight mass on Christmas Eve claim to have witnessed the spectre. Among them is Mr. Chen, a devout member of the church who has lived in Shanghai all his life. He recounts his encounter with the spectre: "I was in the church for the midnight service. As the clock struck twelve, I noticed a figure clad in an ancient robe walking up the aisle. There was a certain solemnity about the figure. I could not see its face, but I could feel an overwhelming presence. It knelt by the altar, as if in deep prayer, and then, it just... vanished."

Then, there is the account of Ms. Wang, a former choir member. She speaks of the spectral figure with a mix of awe and fear. "I saw it first when I was just a child. It was my first midnight mass, and I remember being awestruck by the beauty of the service. And then, I saw it, the figure in the robe. It seemed out of place, and yet, it belonged. It walked slowly, as if in deep contemplation, and disappeared after a moment of prayer at the altar. I have seen it every year since then."

Despite the eerie tales surrounding the shrouded spectre, the congregants of the Holy Trinity church look forward to its spectral visit. To them, it is not a cause for fear but a fascinating part of their Christmas tradition. A reminder of the church's long history, its connection to the unseen, and the timeless mystique of Christmas. As Ms. Wang puts it, "The spectre, to us, is a part of Christmas. It's a tradition, a tale that adds to the spirit of the festival. In its own strange way, it brings us together."

As the city of Shanghai is enveloped in the festive spirit, and the Holy Trinity church lights up for the Christmas service, the tale of the shrouded spectre weaves itself into the tapestry of the city's Christmas lore. A tale that echoes the underlying mystery of the season, a blend of the seen and the unseen, the physical and the spectral, all contributing to the enigmatic charm of a haunted Christmas. And so, as the clock strikes midnight on another Christmas Eve, the congregation awaits the solemn procession of their spectral visitor, a haunting tradition that links them to the spectral realms of the unseen. In the heart of Shanghai's festive celebrations, the spectre continues its silent vigil, a spectral silhouette against the backdrop of the city's oldest church, a haunting echo of Shanghai's Silent Night.

A Scottish Christmas: The Eerie Encounter on the Loch

Tucked away in the Scottish Highlands, cradled amidst steep mountains, lies the mystical Loch Ness. Its dark waters have been the subject of many legends, from tales of monstrous creatures to spectral apparitions. Among these stories, one stands out in its eerie festivity, woven into the tapestry of Christmas folklore. It is a tale that makes its rounds every Yuletide in the small pubs around the Loch and on the hearths of local homes. It is the tale of an uncanny encounter on a frosty Christmas night, aptly named "A Scottish Christmas: The Eerie Encounter on the Loch."

It was Christmas Eve in the year 1885. The residents of the nearby town of Inverness were engaged in festive preparations, their homes warmly lit against the dark, winter night. Among the townsfolk was a local fisherman, Alistair Campbell. A widower, Alistair was known for his quiet and solitary life. His only companion was his faithful dog, a sprightly Collie named Angus.

On this particular Christmas Eve, Alistair and Angus set out on their usual route along the banks of Loch Ness. The calm serenity of the Loch was soothing, its stillness only broken by the occasional lapping of water against the frosty shore. As Alistair cast his nets into the icy waters, Angus sat by, his attentive eyes focused on his master.

As the night grew darker, the quiet of the Christmas Eve was abruptly shattered by a haunting melody that seemed to rise from the depths of the Loch. It was an ancient song, one that resonated with the rhythms of the sea, its melody weaving itself into the winter night. Alistair, taken aback, glanced around to locate the source of the song, but there was no one in sight.

Suddenly, in the dim glow of the moonlight, a figure materialised from the shimmering mist that was hovering over the Loch's surface. It was a woman, her long hair cascading down her shoulders, her eyes as blue as the Loch itself. Clad in what looked like an ancient Celtic gown, she held a harp in her hands, the source of the mesmerising melody that had filled the night air.

Alistair, captivated and fearful in equal parts, watched as the spectral figure moved gracefully over the Loch. Her song grew louder, reverberating through the quiet night. Then, as suddenly as she had appeared, she vanished, leaving behind the lingering strains of her melody and an uncanny calmness.

The tale of Alistair's eerie encounter spread through Inverness, becoming a part of the town's Christmas lore. While some dismissed it as the fanciful tale of a lonely fisherman, many believed in Alistair's spectral encounter. Over the years, several other locals reported similar encounters on Christmas Eve, each account adding a layer to the spectral tale.

A decade after Alistair's experience, another local, a lady named Mairi, recounted her encounter: "I was walking along the Loch on Christmas Eve when I heard a melody. It was so beautiful, so otherworldly. And then, I saw her, the woman on the Loch. She seemed so peaceful, so ethereal. I stood there, listening to her song, till she vanished into the night."

On Christmas Eves, even today, locals and visitors gather around the Loch, the tale of the spectral harpist becoming a part of their Yuletide tradition. As the melody fills the night air, some claim to see the spectral figure on the Loch, her song uniting the living and the spectral in a haunting Christmas celebration.

Through the years, the tale of the spectral harpist of Loch Ness has become an integral part of the Scottish Yuletide folklore. It has grown from being just a local legend to being an eagerly anticipated phenomenon each Christmas. It captures the essence of mystery and beauty that pervades Loch Ness, tying it to the magic of the Christmas season.

Whether the spectral harpist is a ghost or a figment of collective imagination, her tale has transformed a chilly Christmas Eve by a Scottish Loch into a night of enchanting mystery. As the strains of her harp echo over the dark waters of the Loch, the "Eerie Encounter on the Loch" continues to add a spectral charm to the Scottish Christmas, a charm that is as timeless as the Loch itself.

The Possessed Puppet Show of Rome's Piazza Navona

In the heart of Rome, surrounded by Baroque Roman architecture, lies Piazza Navona. Known for its iconic fountains, charming cafes, and vibrant atmosphere, it becomes especially alive during the festive season, with twinkling Christmas lights strung from building to building and cheerful music filling the air. However, among the joyful revelry, a haunting tale persists, one that seems at odds with the festive cheer. It is the tale of the "Possessed Puppet Show of Rome's Piazza Navona."

For generations, puppet shows have been a beloved attraction in the Piazza Navona Christmas Market. Among these shows, one has gained notoriety - the puppet show of Maestro Bartolomeo, a talented puppeteer known for his lifelike marionettes and captivating storytelling.

Bartolomeo's puppet show was no ordinary spectacle. His

marionettes - intricately crafted, colourful figures - captured the hearts of the audience, both young and old. Each Christmas, the locals eagerly anticipated his arrival, his puppet theatre bringing an extra dash of magic to the season.

However, in the winter of 1934, something strange began to occur. It was during one of Bartolomeo's performances, as his marionettes danced and twirled to the merriment of the crowd, when the atmosphere abruptly shifted. The puppet portraying Befana, the witch who is a key figure in Italian Christmas tradition, suddenly came to life, her movements no longer synced with Bartolomeo's strings.

The puppet, to the crowd's awe and horror, began moving independently, her dance turning wild and erratic. Then, in a voice that echoed around the piazza, she began to speak in tongues. The festive air grew heavy, the crowd silenced as the puppet continued her inexplicable behaviour.

Despite Bartolomeo's efforts, he couldn't regain control of the puppet, the strings seemingly useless. In the ensuing chaos, the show was abruptly ended, and the crowd dispersed, whispers of fear replacing the earlier Christmas cheer.

In the days following the eerie event, several audience members reported nightmarish visions and unexplained occurrences. A local baker, Antonio, recalled, "After the show, things were not the same. I would see the Befana puppet in my dreams, hear her voice. It was like she was haunting us."

This paranormal incident marked the end of Bartolomeo's puppet shows. The puppeteer, deeply shaken, packed away his marionettes, vowing never to perform again. The tale of the Possessed Puppet Show of Piazza Navona quickly spread throughout Rome, casting a shadow over the city's Christmas festivities.

The Piazza Navona Christmas Market, once a beacon of holiday joy, became associated with the spectral puppet, the chilling tale serving as a grim reminder of that fateful night. The spot where Bartolomeo's stage once stood remains empty every Christmas, a tribute to the eerie event that took place decades ago.

Despite the passage of time, the story of the Possessed Puppet Show continues to be a part of Rome's Yuletide tradition. During Christmas, as families gather around their hearths, and children listen with wide-eyed wonder, the tale is recounted, a chilling testament to the city's spectral past. The story serves as a stark contrast to the festive cheer, a dark thread in Rome's vibrant Christmas tapestry.

Whether it was the work of an unseen force or merely a product of collective hysteria, the incident remains unexplained. The Possessed Puppet Show of Rome's Piazza Navona continues to fascinate and frighten, its enigmatic mystery adding an eerie layer to Rome's Christmas narrative.

Each Christmas, as lights illuminate Piazza Navona and laughter fills the air, the spectral puppeteer's legacy lives on, a chilling reminder of the puppet show that once delighted crowds and now haunts their memories. The story of the Possessed Puppet Show is now inseparable from the Christmas festivities in Rome, a chilling tale retold each year as a part of the city's Yuletide tradition.

The Ghastly Guest at the Christmas Feast of Rio de Janeiro

In the heart of vibrant Rio de Janeiro, where the rhythm of samba beats against the backdrop of sun-drenched beaches and flamboyant carnivals, there lies a tale as chilling as the snowfall that the city never experiences. This is the tale of the spectral figure seen at the head of a traditional Brazilian Christmas feast – an eerie spectre whose otherworldly presence imbues a deep sense of fear and awe into the hearts of those who have witnessed it.

With a rich history steeped in a tapestry of indigenous, Portuguese, African, and other various influences, Brazil boasts a diverse array of traditions and customs. But none is as universally celebrated as Christmas. As December rolls around, the streets of Rio de Janeiro burst forth in an explosion of light and colour, filled with the jubilant sounds of chorinho and samba suffused with the familiar strains of carols. In the midst of these joyous celebrations, families gather for the grand Ceia de Natal or Christmas supper, laden with colourful dishes that tantalise the senses. But in one old mansion, nestled away in the historic Santa Teresa district, there is one seat that remains eerily vacant – the seat of the spectral guest.

For generations, the Silva family has resided in this grand old house. As per tradition, they celebrate Christmas with a grand feast, inviting friends and extended family members. But there is one rule, as absolute as it is inexplicable – the head of the table remains empty. It's reserved for the spectral guest, a haunting figure seen only on Christmas night.

It was on a balmy Christmas Eve, when the sky was a velvet blanket of stars and the sweet scent of Rabanadas and Bacalhau a Gomes de Sa filled the air, that the first sighting of the spectral guest took place. Great grandfather Alvaro Silva, then a sprightly man full of mirth, was presiding over the Christmas feast. The laughter and chatter around the table died down when Alvaro, whose eyes had grown wide with fear, pointed towards the head of the table. There, shrouded in an ethereal glow, was a figure dressed in attire that harkened back to another era.

Ever since that chilling Christmas, each subsequent generation of the Silva family has reported sightings of the spectral guest, a figure that exudes a sense of quiet melancholy, its eyes reflecting the longing for an era long gone. The spectral guest does not disrupt the celebration but sits in silent observation, seeming to take part in the revelry from a realm beyond the living.

Guests who have seen the spectral figure recall an inexplicable drop in temperature despite the tropical heat. The atmosphere grows heavy, filled with an uncanny sense of dread. The spectral figure is not merely seen but felt. As if, in its presence, the veil between the mortal world and the spectral one becomes thin, leading to a tangible encounter with the supernatural.

There are those who speculate that the spectral guest is the spirit of a Portuguese nobleman, who lived in the mansion during the colonial period and was renowned for his lavish Christmas feasts. Others believe it's the spirit of an indigenous ancestor, who sits at the head of the table to remind his descendants of their roots, even as they partake in a Christian celebration. Despite the numerous theories that abound, the true identity of the spectral guest remains a mystery, adding another layer of mystique to this haunting encounter.

The tale of the spectral guest at the Christmas feast of Rio de Janeiro serves as a poignant reminder of the coexistence of joy and sorrow, celebration and reflection, the mortal realm and the supernatural. As the city of Rio dances and delights in the festive spirit, there is one table where an ethereal figure holds court, a spectral guest that has become as much a part of the Silva family's Christmas tradition as the feast itself.

So, as you celebrate your Yuletide festivities, remember the tale of the spectral guest, a chilling testament to the fact that even amidst the joyous strains of "Noite Feliz" or "Silent Night", there exist corners of the world where the spectral and the festive intermingle, casting a long shadow that ebbs and flows with the Christmas tide.

The Whispers of Warsaw's Snowfall

Warsaw, the capital city of Poland, embodies a history as deep and profound as the wisest of old men. It is a city that has witnessed the turbulence of war, the rise and fall of empires, and the resilience of its people. Yet within the annals of its historical wealth, there exists a tale that weaves itself through the frosty air each Christmas, carried in the quiet lullaby of the first snowfall - The Whispers of Warsaw's Snowfall.

In the very heart of Warsaw's Old Town, a place where history seeps from every cobblestone, and ancient buildings hold countless tales, is Rynek Starego Miasta, or Old Town Market Place. With its ornate structures and colourful facades, it is a hub of festive cheer during Christmas. Yet, as the first snowflakes descend, the air turns thick with anticipation, for it is said that the arrival of the Christmas snow brings with it spectral whispers from the past.

The tale, passed down through the generations, dates back centuries when Old Town was a bustling centre of trade and merriment. Every year, as Christmas approached, the marketplace would don a festive avatar. Shopkeepers would string colourful lanterns, families would gather around hearty meals, and carolers would fill the air with joyful melodies. However, as the first snowflakes fell, a hush would descend upon the market. The ceaseless chatter would give way to an eerie silence, broken only by a murmur that grew louder with each falling snowflake - the Whispers of Warsaw's Snowfall.

The whispers were not like ordinary voices. They held an otherworldly quality, a spectral resonance that sent shivers down the spines of the listeners. At times, the whispers would weave tales of Christmases past, echoing the laughter and merriment of the marketplace. At others, they would recount tales of sorrow and longing, their melancholic tones merging with the soft crunch of snow beneath the feet. It was as if the snow was a canvas, capturing the essence of the city, and the whispers were its painters, crafting stories of a time long gone.

Over the centuries, numerous accounts have attested to these spectral whispers. There is the account of Helena Wójcik, the keeper of a fabric stall in the market in the 18th century. She described the whispers as "gentle as the falling snow yet as tangible as the cold." On one particularly frosty Christmas Eve, she claimed to have heard her name, whispered so clearly it made her drop the silk scarf she was holding.

Then there was the tale of Jan Kowalski, a soldier who returned from war one Christmas in the early 20th century. Seeking the comfort of his city's traditions after the horrors of the battlefield, he found himself in Old Town Market Place as the first snow fell. As he described, the whispers came, soft at first, then growing in intensity until he heard the voice of his fallen comrade, reciting a Christmas toast they used to share. Overwhelmed, he was found weeping in the snow, his tears merging with the whispers of his past.

The whispers continue to manifest to this day. Local resident, Agnieszka Nowak, recalls a Christmas evening not too many years ago when she stood alone in the middle of the snow-filled market. As the whispers began, she heard a lullaby her grandmother used to sing to her on Christmas Eve. Agnieszka, cradling her newborn son, could do nothing but stare in awe at the snowflakes, each one carrying the spectral whisper of her grandmother's voice.

To the people of Warsaw, the Whispers of Warsaw's Snowfall are more than just a tale. They are a spectral tradition entwined in the city's Yuletide celebrations, a haunting symphony that plays only with the arrival of the Christmas snow. Some believe the whispers are the city itself, sharing its stories through the silence of the snowfall. Others claim it to be the echoes of Christmases past, each whisper a testament to the joy, sorrow, love, and longing of those who once walked the city's streets.

So, as Christmas descends upon Warsaw, its citizens watch the skies in anticipation. For with the first snowfall, the festive silence will once again be broken by spectral whispers, recounting tales that seep from the city's ancient stones, carried in the soft lullaby of the falling snow.

In the heart of winter, as the world around plunges into the silence of the season, remember Warsaw. Remember the spectral whispers that dance in its Christmas snowfall, a chilling tale from the world's mystical corners where the spectral world whispers its stories in the hush of the winter wind. For, as the residents of Warsaw would tell you, when the snowflakes descend, history is not just something you read about, it's something you listen to.

The Snowman of the Swiss Alps

In the heart of Europe, where eight alpine countries converge, lies a landscape as mysterious as it is majestic - the Swiss Alps. Nestled amongst these soaring peaks and verdant valleys is an array of picturesque villages, each one boasting unique traditions, vibrant cultures, and captivating folklore. As Christmas time rolls around, these hamlets come alive with festive cheer. However, within this celebratory atmosphere, a chilling tale emerges - that of the enigmatic Snowman of the Swiss Alps.

The story finds its roots in a small mountain village called Graubünden, a settlement as old as the mountains themselves. Known for its rustic charm and friendly inhabitants, the village holds a deep respect for the alpine winter and its manifestations. Yet, when the Christmas snow blankets the village, the air grows thick with anticipation. For the villagers know, the arrival of the snow brings with it an eerie visitor - a snowman that changes its form and location throughout the Yuletide season.

The first mention of this spectral snowman dates back to the mid-18th century, in the diary of a Swiss pastor named Johann Ulrich. In a series of entries around Christmas, Ulrich wrote of a strange occurrence - a snowman appearing in different locations around the village, its form shifting each time it was seen. One day, it took the form of a child playing in the snow; the next, it appeared as an old man bent over with age. As if this shape-shifting weren't chilling enough, Ulrich noted that no tracks led to or from the snowman, its appearance and disappearance as mysterious as the Northern Lights.

Over the years, the tale of the shifting snowman seeped into the fabric of Graubünden's Christmas tradition, each account adding depth to the lore. There was the testimony of Elsbeth Müller, a woman known for her level-headedness, who, in the Christmas of 1892, reported seeing the snowman transform before her eyes from a featureless figure into the likeness of her departed husband. Shocked, Elsbeth could only watch as the snowy apparition tipped its hat to her before resuming its undefined form.

Then, there was the account of Lukas Baumann, a village blacksmith. On a Christmas Eve in the early 20th century, Lukas found the snowman perched atop his roof, peering down at him with icy eyes. As he stared up at it, the figure began to morph, taking on the appearance of Lukas as a young boy. Before he could react, it was gone, leaving behind only a dusting of fresh snow.

In recent years, the eerie phenomenon continues to manifest. Most notably, in 2015, a group of mountaineers on a Christmas trek through the Swiss Alps reported an uncanny encounter. As the sun began to set on Christmas Eve, the hikers noticed a figure in the snow - a snowman that wasn't there before. As they watched, the figure shifted, morphing into the image of a woman, her face etched with sorrow. Taken aback, the mountaineers retreated, the eerie sight of the spectral snowman forever etched in their memories.

To the villagers of Graubünden and those who've encountered it, the Snowman of the Swiss Alps is a spectral entity as enigmatic as the mountains themselves. Its ever-changing form reflects the ever-changing nature of life, its transience a mirror of the fleeting beauty of winter. The phenomenon seems tied to Christmas time, adding an eerie undertone to the village's

Yuletide cheer. Whether a playful spirit or a projection of the villagers' memories, the snowman remains a spectral enigma, a haunting figure that drifts in with the snow, as elusive and captivating as the Swiss Alps themselves.

In a world that often seeks answers, the Snowman of the Swiss Alps stands as a reminder that some mysteries are meant to be savoured, not solved. So, as Christmas descends upon the snow-kissed mountains of Switzerland, remember this chilling tale. For in the quiet, picturesque village of Graubünden, amidst the joyous carols and the warm glow of Christmas lights, a spectral visitor awaits in the snow, an eerie testament to the mysteries that lie in the world's most mystical corners.

The Phantom Carolers of Cape Town

Christmas time in Cape Town, South Africa, is a joyous spectacle. Festive lights glimmer across the city, casting a warm glow over streets lined with old Victorian buildings and modern architectural marvels alike. Palm trees adorned with ornaments sway gently in the summer breeze, the southern hemisphere's response to the traditional Christmas pine. Night markets buzz with activity as Capetonians indulge in holiday shopping, the air filled with the delicious aroma of traditional South African 'braai' and the sounds of vibrant African Christmas carols. However, the cheerful spirit of Christmas also beckons a more haunting presence - the spectral figures known as the Phantom Carolers of Cape Town.

For centuries, the citizens of Cape Town have passed down the tale of these ethereal entities. They are said to make their appearances during the Christmas season, starting on the stroke of midnight on Christmas Eve. These spectral carolers have been heard in various locations across the city, their haunting melodies wafting through the warm African night.

The first documented account of these eerie singers traces back to 1812, in the journal of a British colonial officer named Robert Trench. An unyielding sceptic, Trench was astonished when he found himself woken by the harmonious strains of carolling on Christmas Eve. Following the sound, he was shocked to discover a group of spectral figures singing at the foot of Table Mountain. According to his account, the ethereal choir consisted of individuals of different ages, genders, and racial backgrounds. They sang in perfect harmony, their forms translucent in the moonlight. Trench was so moved by the sight that he committed the tale to his journal, setting the stage for the enduring legend of the Phantom Carolers of Cape Town.

In the years that followed, numerous sightings were recorded, often corroborating Trench's original account. These apparitions did not discriminate by neighbourhood, class, or creed - their ghostly harmonies were reported from the affluent suburbs of Camps Bay to the colourful Bo-Kaap, from the vineyards of Constantia to the bustling city centre. Regardless of where they were heard, the accounts were strikingly similar: a spectral choir, diverse in its make-up, harmonising traditional Christmas carols into the Cape Town night.

In 1968, a notable encounter was reported by a group of university students. In the wee hours of Christmas morning, they heard melodic strains wafting through the corridors of their dormitory. Intrigued, they followed the sound to its source - an ethereal choir, their forms aglow in the moonlight. According to their account, the ghostly choir sang 'Silent Night' in Xhosa, English, and Afrikaans, their voices conveying a sense of peace that transcended the barriers of language and time.

The most recent documented sighting occurred in 2021, when a family residing in Sea Point reported a similar encounter. They had just returned from midnight mass when they heard harmonious singing resonating from their beachfront. There, under the moonlight, they found the spectral choir, their translucent forms glowing against the backdrop of the dark Atlantic waters. Their rendition of 'O Holy Night,' echoing over the rhythmic crash of the waves, left an indelible imprint on the family's Christmas memories.

The Phantom Carolers of Cape Town serve as a spectral reminder of the city's diverse cultural heritage, their ethereal voices a symbol of unity and peace in the festive season. They embody the spirit of 'Ubuntu,' an African philosophy emphasising humanity and interconnectedness. While their presence might be eerie, the spectral carolers have become an integral part of Cape Town's Christmas folklore.

Whether you believe in the tale or not, next time Christmas rolls around, and you find yourself under the star-studded skies of Cape Town, listen closely. Amidst the Christmas cheers and the summer breeze, you might just catch the ethereal notes of 'Joy to the World' or 'The First Noel.' And if you do, remember that you are part of a centuries-old tradition, a spectral serenade transcending the boundaries of life and death, celebrating the spirit of unity, humanity, and Christmas joy in the heart of Cape Town.

The Eerie Echoes of Edmonton's Ice Castle

Each winter, the city of Edmonton in Alberta, Canada, becomes the site of a spectacular icy wonderland. As the season's first snowfall blankets the city, local artists and engineers come together to construct a stunning ice castle, an architectural marvel that attracts visitors from around the world. Intricately carved ice walls, towers reaching up to the sky, and beautiful ice sculptures transform the landscape into a winter wonderland. It's a sight that's as breathtaking as it is cold. Yet, for all its icy beauty, the castle harbours an eerie secret - the haunting whispers of phantom voices, known as the "Eerie Echoes of Edmonton's Ice Castle".

This phenomenon, occurring annually since the inception of the ice castle tradition in the early 2000s, has become an integral part of Edmonton's local folklore. According to numerous accounts, as Christmas approaches, visitors to the ice castle begin to report a strange audial experience - hushed whispers echoing through the castle's icy halls. The voices, it is said, are mostly indistinct, their words unintelligible. Yet, they carry a spectral quality that sends chills down the spines of even the bravest explorers. A ghostly reminder of Christmases past, these voices seem to resonate within the castle itself, their eerie echoes vibrating through the castle's icy walls.

The first documented account of these strange phenomena dates back to 2005, when a group of tourists lodged a formal complaint with the castle's administration about "whispering voices" disturbing their visit. They had assumed it was a prank by other visitors or a sound effect added by the organisers for ambiance. However, the staff was as bewildered as the visitors, as no such sound effects were used in the castle's construction or operation. This was the beginning of a chain of similar incidents reported by visitors every Christmas season, each account as puzzling as the last.

One chilling eyewitness account comes from a local school teacher, Maria Thompson, who visited the ice castle with her class in 2010. As they traversed the labyrinthine corridors of the ice castle, Maria and her students started hearing hushed whispers echoing around them. They assumed it was the wind whistling through the narrow passageways. But as they journeyed deeper into the heart of the castle, the whispers grew louder, forming an eerie chorus of spectral voices. Maria recalls feeling an inexplicable chill running down her spine, her sense of unease intensifying despite the delight of her students at this unplanned "ghostly" experience.

Another intriguing account is from the winter of 2018. An amateur paranormal investigator, Daniel Holmes, after hearing the tales of the eerie echoes, decided to spend a night in the castle in hopes of capturing the spectral sounds. He was not disappointed. As midnight approached, he began hearing the whispers, their soft murmurings echoing through the cold, silent castle. He managed to record these haunting sounds, and though they were mostly unintelligible, one phrase was clear. The voices repeatedly whispered, "In the heart of winter, we return." This phrase, echoing through the cold, icy walls, left Holmes both thrilled and terrified.

The Eerie Echoes of Edmonton's Ice Castle have become an intrinsic part of the Christmas experience in Edmonton. Scientists have attempted to explain the phenomena as acoustic quirks caused by the unique structure of the ice, but these rational explanations have done little to diminish the allure of the ice castle's spectral whispers.

The mystery continues to captivate the imaginations of visitors, adding a spine-chilling thrill to their Christmas celebrations. The icy marvel of Edmonton has become not just a testament to the artistic spirit of humanity but a gathering place for the spectral echoes of Christmases past. Each whisper a haunting reminder of the depth of our historical roots, each echo a resonance of age-old traditions, each voice a phantom recital of the stories that make up the rich tapestry of Edmonton's community.

As each year passes and the ice castle rises again in the heart of winter, the whispers return, adding a ghostly chorus to the city's Christmas carols. They continue to mystify and fascinate, a spectral symphony of voices resonating within the icy walls of the castle, the Eerie Echoes of Edmonton's Ice Castle becoming an eerie, yet enchanting, part of the city's Yuletide lore. So, should you ever find yourself within the frosty grandeur of Edmonton's Ice Castle during Christmas, remember to lend your ear to the wind. Amidst the whispering breeze, you might just catch a phantom echo of Christmases long past.

Yuletide Yokai: Christmas Spirits of Japan

In the land of the rising sun, where ancient traditions meld seamlessly with modern life, there exists a realm where humans and spirits cohabitate. It's the realm of the Yokai, the supernatural entities of Japanese folklore. These are spirits that shape-shift, that beguile and bewilder, sometimes frightful, sometimes benign, but always fascinating.

When it comes to the Christmas season, a time embraced by Japan with fervour and delight, tales of 'Yuletide Yokai' take precedence, adding a touch of the otherworldly to the festive cheer. But these tales aren't the usual stories of reindeer and mistletoe. They are tales of spectral beings causing mischief during the season of goodwill.

One such tale is that of the mischievous 'Kitsune', the fox spirit. While these intelligent beings are known for their trickery throughout the year, they seem to have a fondness for Christmas time. The residents of a small village near Kyoto tell of strange happenings that have become a peculiar part of their Christmas tradition.

Every Christmas Eve, as the story goes, the villagers find their Christmas decorations mysteriously rearranged. Bells from the top of the tree are found at the bottom, candy canes are discovered hanging from rooftops, and presents are found strewn about the yard.

Many villagers report seeing a glowing fox darting through the streets on these nights, a fox with an ethereal aura and intelligent eyes. As one elderly resident, Mrs. Mori, puts it, "It's as though the Kitsune wants to be part of our Christmas, it rearranges but never destroys. We've learned to wake up on Christmas Day and see what the Kitsune has done."

Another Yuletide Yokai tale takes us to the bustling city of Tokyo. Here, amidst the high-tech metropolis, stories persist of the 'Karikimono,' the spirit of unused objects. This Yokai is known to become more active during the Christmas season, a time when many new gifts replace the old.

There are accounts of old Christmas ornaments and decorations moving on their own, turning up in places where they were not initially placed. Mr. Suzuki, a resident of Tokyo, claims, "Last Christmas, I found my old childhood toy, a worn-out teddy bear, sitting under the Christmas tree. I hadn't seen it in years."

Then there's the haunting tale of the 'Yuki-onna,' the snow woman. Often depicted as a beautiful woman with long, flowing hair, clad in white, Yuki-onna is associated with winter and snowy weather. The mountainous regions of Japan, where heavy snowfall is a common sight during Christmas, tell chilling tales of encounters with this icy spirit.

Mountain climbers and hikers have reported eerie sightings of a white figure, disappearing and reappearing amidst the snowstorm. "It was Christmas eve," one climber recounted, "and in the snowstorm, we saw a figure, a woman, standing in the blizzard. She was there one moment, gone the next."

The Yuletide Yokai are an intrinsic part of Japanese Christmas lore. They add a dash of the supernatural to the festivities, making the season even more enchanting. Whether it's the playful Kitsune, the vengeful Karikimono, or the icy Yuki-onna, these tales of spectral beings lend an aura of mystery to the

Christmas cheer in Japan.

But these stories aren't mere folklore. They live in the shared experiences of those who have encountered these spirits, who have found their Christmas turned eerie by the Yuletide Yokai. These tales are shared around Christmas dinners, they echo in the snow-laden streets of Japan, they live in the rustling of the Christmas decorations, and in the echoes of carols sung on silent nights.

As the snow falls softly on Christmas Eve, as gifts are exchanged, and as carols fill the air, remember the Yuletide Yokai. Remember the tales of the Kitsune's tricks, the Karikimono's vengeance, and the Yuki-onna's haunting presence. Remember that in the land of the rising sun, spirits too, celebrate Christmas, in their own uncanny ways. And who knows, perhaps this Christmas, you might have a story of your own to tell, a tale of an encounter with a Yuletide Yokai.

The Bethlehem Phantom: The Holy Land's Christmas Ghost

In the Holy Land, where history and spirituality intertwine, there exist tales as ancient as the land itself. Among these tales, the story of the Bethlehem Phantom is one of the most chilling and fascinating, a spectral entity said to manifest near the ancient city every Christmas.

Bethlehem, the reputed birthplace of Jesus Christ, holds a special place in the Christmas narrative. Yet, amidst the celebratory atmosphere, the air of reverence, and the throngs of pilgrims, lies a tale that adds a dash of the supernatural to the historic city's Yuletide lore.

As the tale goes, every Christmas, when the last stroke of midnight falls, and the Christmas Day dawns, a spectral figure emerges near the Church of the Nativity. It glides silently through the streets of Bethlehem, vanishing as the first rays of the Christmas sun pierce the cold night.

Accounts of encounters with the Bethlehem Phantom are as varied as they are intriguing. Mr. Abdul, a Bethlehem resident, recounts his chilling encounter. "It was a cold Christmas Eve," he said. "As I was returning from the midnight mass, I saw a figure, draped in a shroud, walking towards the Church. It was there one moment and gone the next."

Another account comes from Ms. Maria, a pilgrim who has visited Bethlehem every Christmas for the past 20 years. "There's an air of solemnity that descends on the city at midnight," she says. "And then, you see the phantom, a figure in white, almost glowing in the night. It's eerie but also strangely peaceful."

The most chilling account, however, comes from Father Yosef, a priest at the Church of the Nativity. "I've been serving here for many years," he said. "And I've seen the phantom, more than once. It walks the path from the Shepherd's Field to the Church, like a pilgrim. I've felt a sense of peace, an inexplicable calmness, every time I've seen it."

Over the years, there have been many speculations about the

identity of the Bethlehem Phantom. Some believe it to be a guardian angel, watching over the holy city. Others suggest it might be the spirit of a pilgrim who had come to visit the birthplace of Christ and never left.

But the most intriguing theory suggests that the Bethlehem Phantom could be a manifestation of collective faith and spirituality, a spectral symbol of the deep reverence associated with Bethlehem. As Father Yosef puts it, "It's a reminder of the spiritual essence of Christmas, an echo of the holy past, a symbol of faith."

The story of the Bethlehem Phantom has become an inseparable part of Bethlehem's Christmas lore. It's a tale that adds a spectral dimension to the festive season, a ghostly narrative that intertwines with the spiritual aura of the city.

The Bethlehem Phantom is an uncanny reminder of the city's historic past and its spiritual significance, a spectral figure that walks the holy city every Christmas. So, this Christmas, as you celebrate the joyous occasion, spare a thought for the phantom of Bethlehem. Who knows, you might just catch a glimpse of the spectral figure as it takes its ghostly pilgrimage in the holy city.

The tales of spectral beings and ghostly apparitions remind us that the world is filled with mysteries and wonders beyond our understanding. And among these tales, the story of the Bethlehem Phantom stands out, a chilling, yet fascinating narrative that adds a spectral hue to the joyous Christmas celebration in the Holy Land.

As the clock strikes midnight, and the first light of Christmas Day falls on Bethlehem, remember the tale of the Phantom, the spectral figure that walks the city's ancient streets, a manifestation of faith, history, and the city's enduring spiritual essence. Maybe you'll even decide to go there and see the spectre for yourself one day?

Afterword

As we close the final chapter of "Lee Brickley's Haunted Christmas: Eerie Yuletide Tales from the World's Most Mystical Corners," we are left with a sense of wonder, a feeling of chill, and an eerie excitement that lingers long after the stories have been told. This journey through the uncanny realms of Christmas folklore and the spectral echoes of the holiday season has taken us across the globe, from the frosty shores of Loch Ness to the ancient streets of Bethlehem, and everywhere in between.

The stories compiled within these pages serve as a reminder that the world is much more than it seems, that the veil between the natural and supernatural is sometimes lifted, especially during the time of Christmas. Each story, each tale of eerie happenings and spectral entities, adds a new perspective to our understanding of the holiday season. It emphasises that Christmas, despite its joyous and festive nature, has a spectral side, a haunting beauty that echoes in the chilling winds of winter and the glowing lights of the holiday.

From the ghostly procession in Colonial Williamsburg to the Yuletide Banshee in the Irish Countryside, we've witnessed how folklore, cultural traditions, and ghostly narratives interweave to create a fascinating tapestry of Yuletide hauntings. We've seen how an everyday object like a Christmas tree in Nova Scotia or an Advent calendar in Vienna can become the centrepiece of eerie occurrences. We've journeyed through the spectral landscapes of Christmas, guided by the eerie light of the haunted moon.

Christmas, in all its warmth and joy, is also a time of mystery and ancient folklore, when the barriers between this world and the next become thin, when spectres from the past make their presence known, and when old tales are retold by the fire. This collection of stories serves as a lantern, guiding us through the shadowy corners of Christmas traditions and inviting us to explore the spectral side of the Yuletide season.

While the stories we've shared may be unsettling, they also invite us to reflect on the enduring nature of folklore and the power of stories. They remind us of our shared human need to understand the unexplainable, to face our fears, and to find meaning in the mystical. In the haunting hum of Helsinki, the phantom sleigh bells of Siberia, or the possessed puppet show of

Rome's Piazza Navona, we see reflections of our own hopes, fears, and fascination with the unknown.

As you end this book, it is my hope that these tales have inspired a new sense of wonder and a newfound respect for the spectral beauty of the holiday season. After all, these stories are not just about ghosts, goblins, and eerie happenings; they are about the enduring magic of Christmas, a magic that is as haunting as it is heartwarming.

Thank you for joining me on this spectral journey through the world's most mystical corners. May these eerie Yuletide tales continue to haunt your Christmases, filling them with a sense of wonder, a shiver of delight, and a deeper appreciation for the enchanting mysteries of the holiday season.

Yours in spectral storytelling,

Lee Brickley.

Lee Brickley is a paranormal investigator and author with more than 24 different books currently in publication. If you would like to read more of Lee's work, just search "Lee Brickley" on Amazon. Thank you for buying this book, and Merry Christmas!

Printed in Great Britain
by Amazon